Who needs a therapist?

Therapy book about soul search
Soul Therapy Book for self-exploration and reflection

Colette Mulberry
Author

How to use this book.

This self-exploration therapy book is divided into sessions, and it is recommended to dedicate at least one to two days per question. For example, on day one, you can read the question and contemplate it, making notes as you go. On day two, you can revisit, review, and expand upon your answer.

It's crucial to fully immerse yourself in the process of self-reflection and not rush through the answers. Take the time to sit with the question, delve deep into your soul, and allow yourself the opportunity to resonate with your inner thoughts and feelings.

In the process of self-exploration, individuals may occasionally realize that their preferences are more diverse than initially thought. It's important not to rush to conclusions, as our minds can be conditioned to believe we like certain things. However, upon introspection, one might find that their true inclinations differ from their initial assumptions. Sometimes, we might discover, 'I don't actually enjoy this; I prefer that!' or 'My feelings are not genuine; I've simply been following the easiest path. I truly prefer this!'"

Create a space free from distractions where you can embark on this personal journey of self-discovery. Enjoy this book and may you uncover the profound benefits of soul searching.

What is soul searching?

Soul searching is a way to embarking on a special journey within yourself. It's a profound process that involves deep contemplation and close examination of your true self, your core beliefs, and what holds genuine significance in your life.

During this introspective journey, you delve into your thoughts, emotions, and life experiences, all to gain a deeper understanding of who you truly are. Soul searching often prompts you to ask questions about your values, aspirations, and how your choices and relationships shaped your path until today.

It's a deeply personal adventure that not only helps you uncover more about yourself but also promotes personal growth, allowing you to align with your authentic self.

The book, "Who Needs a Therapist, Soul Search," is authored by Colette Mulberry, a qualified psychiatric nurse, art therapist, and counsellor. In its pages, you'll find guidance and insights to aid you on this transformative journey of self-discovery.

Fully embrace and enjoy this venture!

Colette Mulberry

PART ONE

<u>Getting to know my basic self.</u>

In this chapter, we will delve into the simple yet significant aspects of your life: your favourite colour, foods, drinks, clothing, shoes, hair, makeup, and music. You might wonder why we are focusing on these seemingly basic things. The truth is life often becomes so hectic that we overlook the importance of paying attention to even the simplest elements.

We eat because it is a necessity, we dress because it is expected, and we go through the motions of our daily routines. However, by taking a moment to pause and truly reflect, you can uncover valuable insights about yourself.

I have encountered individuals who express, "I have no idea what colours I like; I just choose whatever is convenient" or "I don't know what food brings me joy; I simply eat to get through the day." Perhaps you have felt this way as well. It could be due to the demands of family life, the pressures of a demanding job, or merely losing touch with your own preferences as time passes.

Regardless of the reasons, the upcoming sessions provide an opportunity to explore these fundamental aspects of yourself. It is a chance to re-establish a connection with your personal preferences and gain a deeper understanding of your identity.

Colour

Colour plays a remarkable role in our lives, shaping our experiences and influencing our emotions. From the vibrant hues of a sunset that evoke a sense of wonder to the soothing tones of a well-designed room that promote relaxation, colour is a powerful force in our daily existence.

It's not just a matter of aesthetics; colour has a profound impact on our mood and well-being. The warm, inviting colours of a cosy home can make us feel safe and content, while the vibrant, energizing colours in a workspace can boost productivity. Colour can also be a form of self-expression, allowing us to convey our personality and individuality through our choices in clothing, decor, and art.

Think about the colours that resonate with you on a personal level. Are there specific shades that bring you joy, calm, or inspiration? Consider the way colour influences your daily choices, from the clothes you wear to the environments you create. By embracing and understanding the value of colour in your life, you can harness its potential to enhance your well-being and bring more vibrancy to your world.

What is your favourite colour, and what does it represent or mean to you? Reflect on the emotions, associations, and significance you personally attribute to this colour. How does it make you feel when you see it or surround yourself with it? Take a moment to explore the impact that colour has on your mood, energy, and overall well-being, and consider how you can incorporate this colour into your surroundings or daily life to enhance your sense of positivity and harmony."

"What colours do you find most calming? Reflect on the colours that evoke specific emotions or sensations within you. How do these colours affect your mood and overall sense of well-being? Take a moment to explore how you can incorporate these calming or energizing colours into your surroundings or daily life to create a more harmonious and uplifting environment for yourself."

We are going to do the same as the previous page, however, we are going to explore an uplifting and energy giving colour!   "What colours make you feel energized and lively? Think about the colours that bring out certain emotions or make you feel a certain way. How do these colours impact your mood and overall well-being? Take a moment to consider how you can bring these energizing colours into your surroundings or daily life to create a more positive and uplifting environment for yourself."

On the previous page we explored your general colour preference, but today we are going to be more specific. "What colours do you prefer to wear in your clothing? Reflect on the colours that make you feel confident, comfortable, or express your personal style. How do these colours influence your mood and the way you present yourself to others? Take a moment to explore how incorporating your preferred colours into your wardrobe can enhance your self-expression and boost your confidence."

Clothing and self-exploration

The clothes we choose to wear can be more than just fabric and fashion; they are a reflection of our inner selves. In the realm of self-exploration, our clothing becomes a canvas through which we paint our identity, values, and emotions. Each outfit tells a unique story about who we are and what we want to convey to the world.

Exploring your relationship with clothing can be a profound journey of self-discovery. It invites you to ponder why you gravitate towards certain colours, styles, or patterns. Do you dress to express your individuality, conform to societal norms, or perhaps seek comfort and confidence? The garments we choose are a mirror reflecting our inner thoughts and feelings.

Moreover, self-exploration through clothing allows us to challenge and reshape our self-image. It's an opportunity to step outside our comfort zones and experiment with new looks that align with our evolving identities. As we sift through our wardrobe, we may uncover hidden aspects of ourselves, rekindle forgotten passions, and, in some cases, even shed layers of the past.

So, whether you're donning your favourite jeans and a t-shirt or dressing up for a special occasion, remember that your clothing choices are an integral part of your self-exploration journey. Embrace them as a tool to express yourself, discover new facets of your personality, and, ultimately, embrace the beautiful complexity of your being.

Are you happy with your current clothing items you wear or does your wardrobe need an update? Do you donate used items to charity, or do you have piles and piles of unused too small or too big items in your wardrobe?

Do you like the clothes you wear, or do you think it's time for a change in your wardrobe? Do you donate clothes you don't need anymore, or do you have a lot of unused items that don't fit you well? Is there enough space in your wardrobe, or is it overflowing? Do you find yourself wearing certain items repeatedly while others just hang there for years? You can open your wardrobe and drawers and give this a deep thought. If change is needed, write a plan for this.

"What type of clothing do you prefer and why? Additionally, explore the colours you favour for this type of clothing."

Did your clothing style change over the years, if so, why, and how does this make you feel, describe your style over time as well.

Shoes

Shoes are more than just things to put on your feet. They can tell a lot about you. Whether you wear sneakers for everyday activities or fancy shoes for special events, your choice of footwear is like a part of your personality.

Different shoes match different parts of your life. For example, tough boots might show that you love outdoor adventures, while fancy shoes could mean you're professional. The colours, materials, and styles you pick say something about your personal taste.

Sometimes, shoes have sentimental value. You might have a pair from a memorable trip, or something passed down from your family. Each step you take in your shoes can remind you of where you've been and what you've done.

When you think about your shoes, it's not just about fashion. It's also about how they show your unique story and how you're finding out more about yourself. So, the next time you put on your favourite pair of shoes, think about what they say about you and how they're part of your life's journey.

"What do your shoes reveal about you and your personality? Reflect on the types of shoes you prefer to wear and the reasons behind your choices. Consider how your shoes reflect your style, values, and the image you want to project. Do your shoes convey comfort, practicality, professionalism, creativity, or a sense of adventure? How do your shoes make you feel and what do they say about your unique identity?"

Is there a particular type of shoe that you admire but haven't had the opportunity to wear, or is it more of a fantasy for you? Take a moment to reflect on why you are drawn to this specific type of shoe and what it represents to you. Consider the occasions or settings in which you imagine wearing them and how it would make you feel. This can be a reflection from years ago as well when you maybe had the opportunity to wear this type of shoes.

Hair

Hair, whether it's short or long, curly, or straight, plays a significant role in how we perceive ourselves and how we're perceived by others. It's more than just strands of protein; it's a source of identity and self-expression.

For many, a great hair day can boost confidence and make you feel like you're ready to take on the world. The way you style your hair can reflect your mood, from a casual, carefree look to a polished, professional one. It's a canvas to experiment with different colours and styles, giving you the freedom to reinvent yourself.

However, it's important to remember that not everyone has hair, and that's perfectly fine. Whether due to medical reasons, age, or personal choice, many individuals embrace baldness or shaved heads with pride and confidence. Hair, or the lack of it, doesn't define your beauty or worth.

For those who have hair, it's a journey of self-expression. For those without it, the choice to embrace their natural state or adopt a style of their choosing is equally empowering. In the end, it's how you feel about your hair or its absence that truly matters. Confidence, self-acceptance, and a positive self-image are what truly shine through, whether you have a head full of hair or not.

"How does your hair contribute to your sense of self-expression and identity? Reflect on the role your hair plays in shaping your self-image, confidence, and personal style. Consider how your hair choices reflect your personality, cultural influences, and values."

Do you have a hairstyle that you really like or find attractive? You can think about past hairstyles you've had or recall a specific memory. Take some time to think about what it is about that hairstyle that you find captivating or interesting. How did it made you feel?

After you spend these two sessions about your hair, do you want to make any changes to your hair, style, or colour? If yes, why do you want to make these changes? Take a moment to think about your reasons and write down a plan with a timeline for when you want to make these changes". If you are happy and content with your hair, you can write here a positive affirmation about your hair, style, and colour.

Make-up

Makeup is a versatile tool that people use in different ways. For some, it's a form of self-expression. It's like painting a canvas, allowing you to show your unique personality through colours and styles. Makeup can be a fun and creative way to tell the world a bit about who you are.

Others use makeup to hide imperfections, like blemishes or dark circles. It's like a little secret weapon that helps boost confidence and make you feel your best.

But, sometimes, makeup can also be like a mask. Some people use it to hide their true feelings or to cover up who they really are. It's important to remember that it's okay to be yourself, with or without makeup. True confidence comes from accepting and embracing who you are, both with and without the cosmetics.

So, whether you love makeup or prefer a more natural look, the key is to be confident in your own skin. Makeup can be a fun addition, but it should never hide the real you.

What are your thoughts on this? How do you feel about makeup and grooming? Take a moment to reflect on your beliefs and why you hold them. Consider how these beliefs influence your own self-image and daily routine.

Whether you choose to wear makeup or embrace a natural look, it's a personal choice that reflects your unique personality. Is there anything you would like to change in this regard? Perhaps you want to gain the confidence to wear less makeup or feel more comfortable applying makeup. Take a moment to write down your thoughts on this matter. Remember, in today's world, there are numerous videos on social platforms that can help you learn techniques and build confidence in your approach to makeup and self-expression. If you are happy as is, discuss your make up or grooming routine.

Nutrition

Food is a blend of taste and texture that goes beyond just nourishment, reaching deep into our very essence. The flavours and sensations it offer can evoke powerful emotions, and the various textures add complexity to the culinary adventure.

But food is more than just a feast for our senses. It connects us to our memories, brings us closer to loved ones, and provides solace in times of need. Cooking becomes a canvas for self-expression, a way to reveal the essence of the cook.

In its simplest form, food is a sensory journey, but it's also a celebration of human existence and a profound expression of our inner selves. Each bite tells a story, and every meal is an opportunity to explore the depths of our souls.

Food is available everywhere, but it requires planning and finances. Let's talk about the types of food you like: homemade, store-bought, or take-out?

If you don't enjoy cooking at home, what's the reason? Lack of time, energy, or skills? Let's explore why and create a plan to address it.

If you enjoy cooking at home, reflect on how you learned and the memories it brings. How does cooking at home make you feel? Write down your thoughts and emotions about the joy of cooking.

Now that you have established what your cooking skill levels are and the reasons behind this, Now let's discuss your food preferences. Do you have any specific dietary preferences or follow a particular eating style such as keto, vegan, or vegetarian? If so, what are the reasons behind your choice? If not, discuss your day-to-day food preferences.

Next, let's explore how you plan your meals. What do you typically include in your meals? Are vegetables, salads, and meats part of your regular choices? Do you enjoy planning and preparing these meals, or do you view them more as a go-to option for your family?

In your journey of self-discovery, let's explore your favourite meal. What is the meal that brings you the most joy and satisfaction? Describe its components and what makes it special to you. Consider the flavours, textures, and aromas that make this meal stand out. How does it make you feel when you indulge in this favourite dish? Reflect on the emotions and sensations it evokes, allowing yourself to fully appreciate the experience.

"What is your favourite drink that brings you comfort and enjoyment? Reflect on the beverage that you find most satisfying and refreshing. This can be any type of drink, hot or cold. Describe its taste, aroma, and the sensations it brings to your senses. Consider the occasions or moments when you often indulge in this drink and how it makes you feel. Does it evoke any memories or special associations? Explore the significance of this favourite drink in your life and how it contributes to your overall well-being."

"What role does alcohol play in your life? Reflect on your drinking habits, frequency, and the reasons behind your alcohol consumption. Consider how alcohol makes you feel and the impact it has on your overall well-being. Are there any concerns or areas for improvement when it comes to your alcohol use? Explore your motivations, values, and the effects that alcohol has on your physical and emotional health. This self-reflection can help you gain a deeper understanding of your relationship with alcohol and identify any changes or adjustments you may want to make for a healthier and more balanced lifestyle."   Do the same exercise if you do not use alcohol at all, describe this in full.

If you're experiencing challenges with alcohol consumption or have realized that you may have a problem; I recommend reading the book "A Sober Life" written by R.E.R. Rowlands. This book offers valuable insights and guidance on living a sober lifestyle. Available online or on request in bookstores.

....

....

....

....

....

....

....

....

....

Self-progression Reflection

Take a moment to summarize what you have learned so far in your self-help journey. Think about how colours influence your life, such as the colours you like, the clothing and colours you wear, shoes, your hairstyle, and your makeup choices. Consider how nutrition and the drinks you consume impact your well-being. Then, provide an overview of your progress and the insights you have gained, highlighting the connections between these different aspects of your life and how they contribute to your overall sense of self.

PART TWO

<u>My own personal journey</u>

In this chapter, we are going to take a close look at who you are—how your entire being is shaped by people and experiences.

We'll begin by exploring your beliefs and what's important to you. You will delve into your thoughts, feelings, experiences, relationships, and choices that have contributed to shaping the person you are today, allowing you to better understand yourself.

As you embark on this journey of self-discovery, it's crucial to recognize that in your pursuit of success, you may inadvertently neglect your own well-being. Self-care and self-love are paramount in this process.

Before you can truly love others, you must first love yourself. By prioritizing self-love, nurturing your own needs, and taking care of yourself, you will discover that you have more quality time and energy to invest in the lives of your loved ones. Not only will you become more confident, but you will also gain a greater sense of control over your own life.

Remember, by giving yourself the attention and care you deserve, you can positively impact both your own life and the lives of those around you.

This is Me

Sometimes there are activities or moments when we feel completely comfortable and happy with who we are. It could be when you're playing a sport, creating art, spending time with friends, playing a music instrument or doing something else entirely. Take a moment to think about that experience. By remembering these moments, you can get a better understanding of what truly makes you happy, fulfilled, and connected to your true self.

....

....

....

....

....

....

....

....

Think about a time when you felt truly like yourself, like the real you. What were you doing at that moment? What made it special? Did you feel free, confident, or genuinely happy?

Think about your hobbies or things that really interest you. What are these interests or hobbies? Consider how these passions and interests shape who you are as a person. Do they help you express yourself, make you feel confident, or allow you to connect with others who share the same interests? How do they make you unique and special? If you want to answer you do not have time for hobbies and interests, write here what you want to do when you have time.

If you had to pick three words to describe yourself, what would they be? And why did you choose those words? Take a moment to think about why you chose those specific words. How do they reflect your personality, your strengths, or the way you interact with others? What makes these words important to you?

Explore your unique interests and their impact on your self-discovery. Identify the areas that truly captivate and intrigue you, whether it's space exploration, history, psychology, technology, animals, or any other subject. Write down three of these interests and reflect on how they make you feel about yourself. Consider how these topics contribute to your sense of identity, connection, purpose, and personal growth. Explore how they shape your perspective and the person you aspire to be.

Thinking about someone you look up to helps you understand the qualities you find meaningful. It shows you the kind of person you want to be and the values you want to have. Writing about them lets you reflect on your own aspirations and the impact they have on you.

Write about someone you admire—a role model or someone famous or close to you. What qualities do they have that you really like? How do those qualities make you feel? Why are they important to you?

Through your life you interact with people which might have helped you grow, taught you important lessons, or supported you during challenging times. It could be a teacher, a friend, or a family member from the past. Take a moment to reflect on which person really made a difference. Think deeply about their influence on you and how they shaped the person you are today.

Write about this person and how they contributed to your life and what you have learned.

Apart from how people affect and shape you, Life is also filled with different experiences that can bring about change, both happy and sad. Now, think about specific events or situations that had a significant impact on you.

Take a moment to reflect deeply on two joyful moments that made a lasting impression on you.

As mentioned on the previous page, life is filled with experiences that can lead to change, both positive and negative. Now, let's shift our focus to challenging times that have had a profound impact on you. However, this time, we will explore the positive aspects that emerged from those situations.

Think about the resilience or strengths you discovered within yourself, as well as any other positive outcomes that arose from those difficult times.

Guiding principles serve as your inner compass. They represent your fundamental beliefs and values, providing you with a moral and ethical framework to stay aligned with what you believe is right. Examples of guiding principles include honesty, kindness, fairness, and personal growth. They help you make decisions that resonate with your values and what truly matters to you.

Now, let's delve deeper into your personal values. Identify at least three values that hold significance for you. Explain why they matter and how you incorporate them into your daily life.

We all want something from life, some people more than other, some is just content with the way life is. Sometimes it is time to stop, sit and think, "am I just chasing a dream all the time and let life passed me?" Or "am I actually working towards something?". If you decide you are content with the way life is, this is ok as well and you can work to live and not live to work.

Think about what you want from life. What are your dreams, goals, and hopes? Write about what you expect from life and why it's important to you.

Review your life expectations from the previous page and write down how you actively work towards your expectations. Do you need to make any changes to achieve them? If yes, identify what needs to change and write down ideas on how to make those changes. If no changes are needed, describe how these expectations bring value to your current life and future.

Self-Love

Self-love is about mindset and to embrace and care for yourself unconditionally. This means treating yourself with kindness, compassion, and respect. It involves recognizing your worth, embracing your strengths and flaws, and prioritizing your well-being and happiness.

Explore what self-love means to you and why it's important. Reflect on how you take care of yourself and the positive impact it has.

Explore the areas of your life where you may need more self-love and understand how it affects your overall well-being. By exploring this, you can learn how to take better care of yourself and show yourself the love you deserve.

Self-love includes to accept yourself as you are, to surround yourself with only positive influences to set boundaries and to be aware that self-love is an ongoing journey which require ongoing participation, effort, and patience. This is also a deeper, long-term practice of valuing and respecting yourself.

Think of practical ways to nurture self-love and self-care in your daily life.

Self – Care

Self-care which forms a part of self-love is about your immediate needs and long term needs to stay mentally and physically healthy as you grow older. This is basically to take care of your overall well-being.

As self-love focusses on the unseen, self-care focusses on specific actions and practices taken to promote, mental, physical, and emotional well-being. This involves things like participating in exercising and activities which bring joy and relaxation, enough sleep, eating healthy food as well as spending time with family members.

How do you incorporate self-care in your life? Is there anything you want to change? What else can you do?

Ways of Wellbeing

Wellbeing is not a one-size-fits-all concept; it's about recognizing that there are different paths to personal contentment and fulfilment. Embracing diverse ways of wellbeing allows individuals to tailor their approach to what truly nourishes their mind, body, and spirit. Whether through physical exercise, mindfulness, social connections, creative expression, or other avenues, the beauty of these varied paths lies in their ability to empower people to find what resonates most with their unique needs and aspirations, ultimately leading to a more balanced and satisfying life.

Therefore, another aspect of self-care involves focusing on well-being. In this section, we will explore six well-being strategies that can benefit both your physical and mental health.

What do you consider to be essential components of well-being? Share your thoughts here on what you believe well-being should encompass.

....

....

....

....

....

....

....

Ways of Wellbeing

1. Connect and engage with other people.

Relationships help you feel like you belong and are accepted. They also give you a chance to share good experiences with others.

Here are some ways to connect and engage with other people:
A. **Empathetic Connection**: Use Empathy to connect with others and use this skill to build strong, meaningful relationships.
B. **Eye Contact**: Adequate eye contact is inviting and comforting to others. Maintain this genuine connection with your eyes.
C. **Being Present**: Be fully present in the moment. Stay mindful of keeping distractions at bay to give your undivided attention.
D. **Genuine Body Language**: Try to be yourself. Your genuine smiles and gestures make people feel at ease and accepted.
E. **Respect for Differences**: Acknowledge that diverse perspectives are a strength. Embrace this and learn from the differences.
F. **Common Ground**: Seeking shared interests and experiences will help deepen your relationships.
G. **Remembering Names**: The ability to recall people's names makes people feel valued and respected.
H. **Balanced Sharing**: Have a sense of balance in sharing personal information, do not overshare. Sharing experiences (without trying to compete) fosters an environment of trust and mutual disclosure.

I. **Patience in Building Connections**: Understand that building meaningful connections can take time. Be patient and let relationships develop organically.

J. **Thoughtful Follow-Ups**: Following up is a way to show you care and are invested in people. Keep reaching out to maintain connections and nurture relationships.

Remember, engaging with people is a journey of growth and learning. Your unique qualities and characteristics will continue to evolve and refine your ability to connect with others in meaningful ways.

How do you engage with people on a regular basis? Do you participate in engaging in your local community? Please describe and if you don't, write ideas of how to start engaging.

2. <u>Continuous learning</u>

By now, most people realize the importance of an active mind. The old saying of "you are never too old to learn" has never been truer! Learning and keeping your brain active is important because it helps you stay sharp, adaptable, and engaged with the world. It improves your thinking, memory, problem-solving skills, and creativity. Lifelong learning keeps your mind flexible, promotes personal growth, and helps you handle life's challenges and changes better.

Continuous learning is a lifelong journey that can take many forms. Here are a few examples:

A. **Online Courses and Webinars**: Explore various platforms to acquire new knowledge and skills in a wide range of subjects.
B. **Reading**: Read a variety of books, fiction, non-fiction, and self-help, to expand your horizons and stimulate your mind.
C. **Podcasts**: Tune in to educational podcasts on topics of interest to you, learning from experts and thought leaders.
D. **Artistic Pursuits**: Dive into the arts, whether it's painting, music, or writing, as a creative form of self-expression and learning.
E. **Cooking and Culinary Skills**: Enhance your culinary abilities by experimenting with new recipes and techniques.
F. **Meditation and Mindfulness**: Develop a daily mindfulness or meditation practice to promote emotional well-being and self-awareness.
G. **History and Culture**: Study the history and culture of different regions and time periods to gain a broader perspective on the world.

H. **Travel and Exploration**: Travel to new places, experiencing diverse cultures and expanding your understanding of the world.

I. **DIY Projects**: Engage in DIY (Do It Yourself) projects to learn practical skills in areas like home improvement, electronics, or woodworking.

Do you keep your mind active by learning? If so, what do you do and about what topics? Also, what other areas would you like to explore? If you don't, why not and how can you change this, about what would you like to learn? This can be anything under the sun!

3. <u>Get moving!</u>

Excursive offers benefits that extend far beyond fitness. Exercise is not only good for your body but also for your mind. The "feel-good factor" associated with exercise is closely tied to the release of endorphins, which are natural mood lifters. Therefore, regular physical activity can reduce stress, anxiety, and depression while promoting a sense of well-being and happiness.

Additionally, exercise can also enhance self-esteem, improve sleep, boost energy levels, and increase overall vitality. So, while exercise certainly contributes to physical fitness, its positive impact on mental and emotional well-being is equally significant, making it a powerful tool for enhancing the quality of life.

There are many ways to exercise, like going to the gym, walking in your neighbourhood, going to the park, doing workouts at home, walk in nature, swimming and even chair exercises for older adults

Do you currently exercise? If so, what do you do, please describe and is this enough, or how can you improve? If you don't exercise at all, what can you do to change this?

....

....

....

....

....

4. <u>Give</u>

To give is to be present in other people's lives. Support a local food bank, donate clothing to your charity, give your time for helping in the community, bake cakes for a bake sale.

Remember, giving to others can come in many forms, big or small, this does not need to include money. The most important thing is to approach it with a genuine desire to make a positive difference in someone's life.

To give your time can also mean giving to yourself. It's essential to take care of your own well-being before you can effectively support others. When your intention is to give back to the community, make sure you prioritize spending quality time with your family first. They should never receive second best; family comes first, as they are the fundamental building blocks of our society. A mere half an hour of dedicated, phone-free quality time can be more meaningful than hours of divided attention.

Another way to get family involved, Is to give together as a family your time, if you are alone, you do this on your own.

A. **Volunteer**: Offer your time and skills to local organizations, charities, or community centres.
B. **Educational Initiatives**: Volunteer in schools, libraries, or community centres to help with educational programs or tutor students.
C. **Neighbourly Acts**: Simple acts of kindness, like helping neighbours with yard work or providing assistance during times of need, can make a significant difference.
D. **Donating Goods**: Donate clothing, toys, or other items to organizations that distribute them to those less fortunate.

E. **Animal Welfare**: Volunteer at local animal shelters or rescue organizations, fostering animals, or helping with their care.

Remember, the key to successful community involvement is finding opportunities that align with your interests, skills, and availability. Your contributions, no matter how small, can make a significant difference in your community and create a more connected and vibrant society.

How do you give in your everyday live and community? If you don't, how can you participate? Can you clean out your wardrobe or volunteer? Explore this topic.

<u>Live mindful</u>

Be present. Put the phone down and take in what is going on around you. Forget the "likes" on Facebook! Going for a walk? Keep your phone in your bag, explore the area, see the environment, touch the leaves, and smell the air.   There is no need to take photos of literally everything! Take memory photos with your mind.

"Memory photos" is a powerful concept that encourages us to capture moments with our eyes and mind, rather than through the lens of a mobile phone. It invites us to fully immerse ourselves in the present, to practice mindfulness, and to embrace life as it unfolds in its raw and unfiltered beauty. These "memory photos" serve as a reminder to experience every facet of life – the joy, the serenity, the melancholy, and even the challenges.

 It's an invitation to absorb the essence of every moment, to savour life's rich tapestry, and to appreciate the profound depth of each experience. It's about drinking in the world around us, living it fully, and creating a treasury of memories that transcend the limits of any photograph.

Be present. Put the phone down and take in what is going on around you. Forget the "likes" on Facebook! Going for a walk? Keep your phone in your bag, explore the area, see the environment, touch the leaves, and smell the air.   There is no need to take photos of literally everything! Take memory photos with your mind.

What do mindfulness mean to you? How do you practice this and
if not, write down ideas how to practise this.

5. <u>Break free from technology.</u>

Finding balance in technology usage is crucial for overall well-being. Mindless scrolling and excessive information consumption can lead to anxiety and restlessness. Reflect on your own habits of mindless scrolling and consider why you engage in this behaviour and what you gain from it. Explore alternative activities that can replace mindless scrolling and promote a healthier relationship with technology.

However, keep in mind that, even when you're just scrolling through online content, it can be a good idea to look for uplifting stuff. It helps balance out the negative things you might come across online. Positive content can boost your spirits and remind you that challenges are temporary, and you have the potential for growth and happiness. So, by enjoying uplifting posts while scrolling, you can feel better and more motivated."

The question can be, how to start unplugging and break free from technology. A starting point can be to schedule regular "unplugged" periods in your day, where you intentionally put away your devices and engage in activities like reading a physical book, going for a walk, or having face-to-face conversations. This practice can help you disconnect from the digital world and reconnect with the real one. Keep a schedule to help you, depending how attach you are to technology.

Another idea to break free from technology is to allocate zones in your home where no technology is allowed, this can be the dining room or bedroom. These areas can serve as sanctuaries where you focus on non-digital activities, fostering a healthier balance between your online and offline life.

When you're scrolling online or on social media, what kind of content do you typically gravitate towards? Is there anything you'd like to modify about your online habits? This might involve reducing your online time, outlining your approach to this change, or exploring different websites.

Like the prior question, but how does this content support your personal development and overall happiness? Think about the beneficial influence it exerts on your life and how it resonates with your principles and passions.

6. <u>Paying it forward</u>

"Pay it forward" means doing something kind or helpful for someone without expecting anything back. The idea is that they will then do something kind for someone else. It's like creating a chain of kindness that keeps going and helps many people. It can make a difference in someone's life, strengthen communities, inspire others to be kind, and bring personal fulfilment and happiness.

In your journey of self-improvement, how can you practice the art of "paying it forward"? Reflect on a particular instance when you did just that and share your insights and experiences.

Self-progression Reflection

In this section of the book, take a moment to reflect and summarize what you have learned so far. Identify the areas where you can show more love and kindness to yourself and explore different ways to incorporate self-care into your life. Consider the various aspects of your well-being, such as physical, emotional, and mental health, and how they contribute to your overall happiness. Additionally, reflect on the importance of paying it forward and spreading kindness to others. Summarize your insights and create a roadmap for nurturing self-love, practicing self-care, and promoting well-being in your daily life.

PART THREE

<u>The Soul.</u>

Faith, hope, and spiritual awareness.

Discovering faith, hope, and something to believe in is a profound journey that extends beyond our physical and mental well-being. It delves into the realm of the unseen, the spiritual world that exists alongside our physical existence. While we cannot see or fully comprehend this spiritual aspect, we are aware of its presence. We are complex beings, composed of countless cells, each contributing to our unique mind, body, and soul.

As we explore our inner selves, it's essential to reflect on the health of our soul, the part of us that is unseen and unheard. Do we believe in a higher power? Have we delved into the literature surrounding spiritual matters? These questions lead to countless debates and inquiries. Personally, I have found that giving life purpose involves striving for something beyond the confines of our mortal existence. It means working towards an everlasting life.

Does such an existence truly exist? The answer may only be revealed beyond the veil of death. However, it is wise to approach life with preparation and faith rather than being helpless and devoid of belief.

Faith, by its very definition, is the belief in something we cannot see. I, for one, embrace faith and refrain from judging those with differing beliefs. Discovering a higher power to believe in is vital; it grants meaning to our earthly existence. Remember, the journey of finding faith is deeply personal and introspective.

Journaling about this process allows us to explore our own beliefs and deepen our spiritual connection.

Rooted believes.

Reflect on your beliefs: Begin by reflecting on your current beliefs and understanding of faith. What does faith mean to you? How has it played a role in your life, if at all? Consider any experiences, questions, or doubts you may have had in relation to faith.

Express your desires and questions: Write down any desires or questions you have regarding faith. What are you seeking or hoping to find? What aspects of faith are important to you? Consider any doubts or uncertainties you may have and allow yourself to express them openly.

The journey of faith

Faith for some a sensitive matter, for others an interesting point of discussion, and for others non – existent. Whatever your take on faith, be open to new perspectives and ideas as you explore faith. Be patient with yourself on this lifelong journey, knowing that beliefs can change and grow.

Express your thoughts and emotions freely in your journal without judgment. Let it be a safe space for reflection and personal growth as you follow your own unique spiritual path.

Explore your spiritual journey: Write about your personal spiritual journey and any experiences that have influenced your quest for faith. This can include moments of inspiration, encounters with different beliefs or traditions, or significant life events that prompted deeper reflection.

Sense of connection or spiritual presence: Reflect on how these experiences contribute to your understanding and exploration of faith.

Seek guidance and inspiration: Read spiritual texts, books, or seek guidance from mentors, spiritual leaders, or communities that resonate with your interests. Note any insights, teachings, or quotes that inspire you and reflect on how they relate to your own journey.

Cultivate practices and rituals: Explore different practices and rituals that align with your desire to find faith. This could include prayer, meditation, journaling, attending religious services, or engaging in acts of service and compassion. Write about your experiences with these practices and how they impact your sense of faith.

<u>Self-progression Reflection.</u>

As you reflect on the past few sessions and your exploration of finding faith, consider what you found to be meaningful and significant. What aspects resonated with you and felt important in your journey? Looking ahead, what is your vision for your faith path? How do you envision deepening your spiritual connection and incorporating your newfound insights into your daily life? Take a moment to contemplate your path ahead and the steps you can take to continue nurturing your faith.

PART FOUR

Fear, Relaxation, Relationships and Gratitude.

Fear

Fear is a small word but contain different meanings for different people. There are many types of fear. Fear is a natural part of being human and serves as a protective mechanism. It can manifest in various forms, ranging from fears related to immediate physical danger that activate our 'fight-or-flight' response, to fears rooted in past experiences, such as post-traumatic stress disorder. You can also experience fear of change and fear for the unknown. This type of fear can sometimes be a hinderance for progress and not a tread.

While fear can be a normal human experience, it can also become overwhelming and extend its influence beyond yourself. You may unknowingly transfer your fears to your children, hindering their ability to fully embrace life and limiting their potential, all due to apprehension of the unseen.

The fear of the unknown can hold you back from taking the next step, whether it involves stepping outside your comfort zone or making a career change.
Fear encompasses multiple aspects, including both rational and irrational fears that can impact our lives in various ways.

Being able to identify misplaced fears may help you overcome or at least manage misplaced beliefs and fears, which can result in panic attacks.

When exploring fears and the intense physical sensations, such as an increased heart rate, rapid breathing, and sweating that accompany a panic attack, it is important to understand that these are part of a physiological reaction involving an adrenaline surge. With this knowledge, you can begin to manage and cope with the any form of anxiety and panic.

Write about an experience that caused you fear or anxiety. Reflect on how it impacted you and what you learned from facing that fear.

Explore a fear or limiting belief that holds you back. How can you reframe this belief or take steps to overcome it?

Identify a fear that seems irrational or illogical to others but is significant to you. Explore the origins of this fear and why it has such a strong hold on you.

Write about a fear you would like to overcome. What steps can you take to challenge and conquer this fear? Visualize yourself overcoming it and imagine how it would feel.

Write a letter to your fear. Express your thoughts, frustrations, and intentions to overcome it. Challenge your fear and affirm your determination to move beyond its grip.

Reflect on the impact of fear on your life. How has it limited you or prevented you from fully embracing opportunities or experiences? Write about the changes you would like to see by confronting your fears.

....

....

....

....

....

....

*Note for Thought**

Our fears can impact not just ourselves but also those around us, including our children. They can shape how our children perceive the world, make choices, and seize opportunities. When we let our fears influence our parenting, we may unknowingly limit our children's potential and hinder their growth. It's crucial to recognize the impact of our fears on our children and create an environment of support and empowerment. By facing our fears and fostering resilience, self-belief, and fearlessness, we can inspire our children to pursue their dreams confidently. Take a moment to reflect on how your fears may be affecting your children and explore ways to encourage their strength and confidence.

<u>Relaxation</u>

Incorporating relaxation and calm into your daily life is crucial for your well-being. Whether it's taking an hour during the day to peacefully enjoy your lunch or setting aside an hour at night to unwind and destress, even a small amount of dedicated time is better than none.

Relaxation helps clear your mind, refresh your brain, and serves to address stress and restlessness. Make it a priority to create moments of relaxation in your day-to-day routine for a healthier and more balanced life. There are numerous ways to incorporate. relaxation into your daily routine. As mentioned, you can find peace and tranquillity by enjoying your lunch in a calm environment or by taking a moment to unwind with a cup of coffee or your favourite non-alcoholic drink.

Engaging in activities like reading, adult colouring (which has its own set of benefits), practicing physical relaxation exercises, or even taking a power nap can also contribute to your overall relaxation. Explore different methods and find what works best for you in creating moments of relaxation throughout your day.

"What are some activities or practices that help you unwind and relax after a long day? Reflect on the methods you currently use or have used in the past to promote relaxation and calmness. How do these activities make you feel, and what benefits do they bring to your overall well-being?

"What is one area of your life where you often feel overwhelmed or stressed? Reflect on how this affects your well-being and consider what relaxation techniques or strategies you could incorporate to alleviate these feelings.

How can you create moments of calm and rejuvenation within your daily routine to counterbalance stress? Explore different activities or practices that resonate with you, such as meditation, journaling, nature walks, or engaging in hobbies. Write down your ideas and develop a personalized relaxation plan to nurture your mental and emotional well-being."

<u>Relationships</u>

Relationships come in various shapes and forms, but they all share one common element: the emotions they evoke, be it positive or negative. Relationships have the power to lift you up, bringing happiness and joy, or they can become toxic and harmful. Unfortunately, many individuals, both women and men, who find themselves in toxic relationships often.
believe it is their own fault or feel trapped.

In the upcoming sessions, we will delve into the topic of relationships. If you find yourself in a toxic situation, it is highly recommended to seek help and advice to navigate through this challenging experience. Remember, you deserve to be in healthy and supportive. relationships that contribute positively to your well-being.

On a more positive note, and as mentioned before, relationships have the potential to be incredibly uplifting and fulfilling, providing a sense of purpose and connection to both individuals and local communities.

Building strong relationships can enhance your overall well-being, offering support, companionship, and a sense of belonging. By nurturing positive relationships, you can experience greater happiness, emotional support, and a network of individuals who share your values and interests.

Whether it's with friends, family, a romantic partner or community connections, investing in healthy and meaningful relationships can bring immense joy and fulfilment to your life.

Firstly, we are going to Explore the different types of relationships in your life and gain insights into the dynamics that shape them.

"Identify two relationships in your life that brings you joy, support, and a sense of positivity? Reflect on the qualities and dynamics of this relationship that make it so meaningful to you. How does this person uplift and inspire you? Take a moment to appreciate the positive impact this relationship has on your well-being."

Explore the impact of your social circle on your well-being and if you need to nurture existing relationships or need to build connections with similar interests to expand your social circle, discover strategies for building a supportive network of friends and loved ones.

"What is one negative influence or toxic relationship in your life that drains your energy and impacts your overall well-being? If this is not a person, it can be a situation. Reflect on the behaviours, attitudes, or actions of this person / situation that have a detrimental effect on your happiness and personal growth. How does this negative person / situation impact your self-esteem and emotional state? Take a moment to consider strategies for setting boundaries, minimizing interactions, or seeking support to protect your well-being and create a more positive environment for personal growth."

"What are your expectations from a meaningful and fulfilling relationship? Take a moment to reflect on what qualities, values, and experiences you desire in your ideal relationship. Consider the emotional support, communication, trust, and shared values that you believe are essential for a healthy connection. How do these expectations align with your personal growth and overall well-being? Reflect on what you are willing to contribute to foster a fulfilling relationship that meets your expectations."

Relationship with my work

What is the most enjoyable work or activity you have engaged in throughout your life? It could be something from years ago. Reflect on the aspects of that work that brought you joy and fulfilment. Is there a way to reintroduce elements of it into your current daily life?

What are your hopes and dreams when it comes to the things you do each day, whether it's your job or the tasks you perform in your daily life? Reflect on what truly brings you joy and fulfilment. If you are unhappy in your current work/life environment, think and delve deep and try to find at least one positive point.

Think about the factors that contribute to your work / day to day satisfaction, like finding a good balance between your work and personal life, feeling a sense of growth and progress, and doing things that align with your passions and values. How do these expectations contribute to your overall happiness and well-being? Take a moment to imagine your ideal situation and think about the small steps you can take to bring your daily activities closer to your aspirations."

"What is one aspect of your work / life that consistently drains your energy and causes dissatisfaction? Reflect on the negative impact it has on your well-being and overall job satisfaction. How does this issue affect your motivation and productivity? Take a moment to identify potential steps you can take to address or mitigate this negative work-related issue and improve your overall work experience."

Consider a type of work or activities you would like to pursue that are different from your current job or situation. What aspects of these activities appeal to you? Can you explore ways to incorporate them into your life, whether it's through hobbies, volunteering, or exploring new career paths? Take a moment to envision how you can bring more of this desired work into your daily life and consider the steps you can take to make it a reality.

Gratitude

Gratitude is about noticing and appreciating the good things in life, whether they are big or small. It means saying 'thank you' for the good moments and the blessings we have.

When we practice gratitude, we shift our attention from what's missing or going wrong to what's going well. This positive focus helps us feel happier and more content. Gratitude is like a superpower that boosts our resilience and helps us find joy in everyday life.

To incorporate gratitude into your daily routine, consider keeping a gratitude journal. Each day, write down three things you are thankful for. They can be as simple as a warm cup of coffee in the morning, a kind word from a friend, or the beauty of nature. Reflecting on these moments of gratitude can enhance your overall sense of well-being.

Additionally, take a moment to express your appreciation to others. A heartfelt 'thank you' can strengthen your relationships and spread positivity. Practice mindfulness by being present in the moment and savouring the good experiences.

Remember, gratitude is a powerful tool for cultivating happiness and resilience, so make it a part of your daily life."

"What are two things in your life that you are grateful for? Reflect on the positive aspects, people, or experiences that bring you a sense of gratitude and appreciation. How do these things enrich your life and contribute to your overall well-being? Take a moment to express your gratitude and contemplate how practicing gratitude can positively impact your perspective and daily life."

"What is one small act of kindness or gesture from someone that you are grateful for? Reflect on the impact it had on you and how it made you feel. How did this act of kindness enhance your day or bring positivity into your life? Take a moment to express your gratitude for this specific act and consider how you can pay it forward by spreading kindness to others."

"What is something small in your everyday life that you sometimes forget to appreciate, but actually brings you comfort, joy, or a peaceful feeling? It could be a simple moment or an ordinary thing. How does recognizing and being thankful for these little pleasures make you feel happier and more content? Take a moment to express gratitude for this specific part of your daily life and think about how you can remind yourself to be more grateful for the small things in your day-to-day experiences."

<u>Self-progression Reflection.</u>

Reflect on the discoveries you've made in this part of the book, focusing on beliefs, faith, spiritual encounters, and moments of inspiration. Consider the impact of fear, anxiety, and the limiting beliefs that have held you back. Explore the dynamics of your relationships, both positive and negative, and how they influence your well-being. Reflect on the balance between work and life and the importance of finding harmony. Lastly, contemplate the power of gratitude in your life and how it can enhance your overall sense of fulfilment. Summarize your findings on these topics, capturing the insights and growth you've experienced along the way.

PART FIVE

<u>Other joys of life!</u>
Music, Gardening, Books and Art

Engaging with music, flowers, and books can have profound benefits for the soul.

Music has the power to uplift our spirits, evoke emotions, and transport us to
different emotional landscapes. It can soothe our worries, energize us,
or provide a sense of catharsis.

Flowers, with their beauty and vibrant colours, can bring joy, serenity, and a connection to nature. They can uplift our mood, inspire creativity, and enhance our overall well-being.

Books, on the other hand, offer a gateway to different worlds, knowledge, and perspectives. They can ignite our imagination, expand our understanding, and provide solace and wisdom.

These three elements can nourish our soul, providing moments of beauty, inspiration, and reflection that bring us closer to ourselves and the world around us.

<u>Music</u>

"What role does music play in your life? Reflect on how music makes you feel, the emotions it evokes, and the impact it has on your well-being. Consider the genres, artists, or songs that resonate with you and why. How do you incorporate music into your daily routine or special moments? Take a moment to explore the power of music in your life and how you can harness its benefits to enhance your mood, motivation, and overall sense of joy and connection."

"What is a song or musical piece that brings you joy or uplifts your mood? Reflect on the emotions and memories associated with this music. How does it make you feel when you listen to it? Take a moment to appreciate the power of music in enhancing your well-being and consider incorporating more of these positive musical experiences into your daily life."

What kind of music or songs do you listen to when you're feeling sad? Think about the emotions that these musical choices evoke in you. How does the music help you understand and deal with your feelings? Take a moment to explore how music can heal and uplift your mood.

....

....

....

....

....

....

....

....

....

Note for thought *

Listening to uplifting music when you feel down can have a positive impact on your mood and well-being. Upbeat and positive music has the power to uplift your spirits, boost your energy levels, and shift your focus towards more positive thoughts and emotions. It can help you break free from negative thought patterns and provide a sense of comfort and inspiration. By choosing uplifting music, you create an environment that supports your emotional well-being and promotes a more positive outlook on life.

Green Fingers!
The hidden power of flowers, plants, and gardening

The presence of flowers and plants in our lives offers a wealth of benefits that extend far beyond their aesthetic appeal. Engaging in gardening provides a therapeutic avenue for stress relief. The act of tending to a garden, whether it's a vibrant collection of flowers or a serene bed of lush greenery, allows us to reconnect with nature, offering a respite from the hustle and bustle of modern life.

Gardening becomes an opportunity to escape the pressures and demands of daily routines, allowing us to immerse ourselves in the simple yet profound act of nurturing life. This connection with the earth can be a source of tranquillity, helping to calm our minds and reduce stress levels.

Moreover, the act of gardening is a form of self-expression, enabling us to shape and nurture a space that is uniquely ours. It fosters a sense of ownership, accomplishment, and pride in the growth and development of the plants we cultivate. The act of caring for living things and witnessing their growth not only imparts a sense of responsibility but also bolsters our self-esteem and self-worth.

It's a good way to witness the positive impact of our efforts, which, in turn, boosts our overall sense of well-being. The benefits of flowers and plants in our lives, along with the therapeutic practice of gardening, are a testament to the profound connection between nature and our personal growth and contentment.

"What flowers or plants bring you a sense of joy, calmness, or connection to nature? Reflect on the feelings and emotions that certain flowers evoke within you. How can you incorporate these flowers or plants into your environment to create a more uplifting and peaceful space? Take a moment to explore the beauty and symbolism of flowers and consider how they can positively impact your well-being and overall sense of harmony."

"What role does gardening play in your life, what interests you about gardening or if you never planted or gardened before, discuss why have you never tried? Reflect on the benefits and enjoyment you already experience or can experience from nurturing plants and being in nature. How does or can gardening contribute to your well-being and sense of connection? Reflect on the positive impacts that gardening can have on your overall journey of self-discovery and how it can contribute to your personal growth and well-being".

"How can you incorporate gardening into your life and daily routine? Reflect on the possibilities of integrating gardening activities into your schedule, whether it's tending to indoor plants, creating a small garden on your balcony, or dedicating time to a backyard garden. Consider the benefits of nurturing plants and being in touch with nature. How can gardening bring more balance, peace, and joy to your life? Take a moment to explore practical ways to incorporate gardening into your lifestyle, making it an enjoyable and fulfilling part of your self-care and personal growth journey."

....
....
....
....
....
....

... <u>*Note for thought*</u> *

Gardening holds hidden powers that go beyond simply growing plants. It can nurture our well-being, promote mindfulness, and foster a deeper connection with nature. Through the act of tending to plants, we tap into a sense of purpose and responsibility, experiencing the satisfaction of witnessing growth and transformation. Gardening also provides a space for relaxation and stress relief, allowing us to escape the hustle and bustle of daily life and find solace in the beauty of nature. Moreover, it teaches us patience, resilience, and the importance of caring for something outside of ourselves. The hidden powers of gardening lie in its ability to cultivate not only thriving gardens but also personal growth, mindfulness, and a profound appreciation for the wonders of the natural world.

Books

Books have a unique ability to captivate our minds and transport us to different worlds. They can provide us with knowledge, inspiration, and a sense of connection. Whether it's a storybook that sparks our imagination, a self-help book that offers guidance and insights, a magazine that informs and entertains, or an adult colouring book that promotes relaxation and creativity, books hold a special place in our lives.

"What books or genres do you find most uplifting and empowering? Reflect on the books that have inspired you, motivated you, or provided valuable insights into your life. How can you prioritize reading books that align with your personal growth and well-being? Take a moment to consider how intentional reading can support your self-help journey and help you cultivate a positive mindset, gain new knowledge, and find guidance on your path to self-discovery and personal fulfilment".

"Reflect on the genres, authors, or specific books that have impacted you and helped you on your journey. How can you incorporate more intentional reading habits into your daily life to expand your knowledge, gain new perspectives, and find inspiration? Take a moment to consider how books can serve as a valuable tool for self-discovery, personal growth, and enhancing your overall well-being."

Reflecting on the role books play in your life can reveal their impact on your personal growth and well-being. Consider how books have expanded your knowledge, shaped your perspectives, or provided comfort during challenging times. Explore the emotions and experiences that books evoke within you and how they contribute to your overall sense of fulfilment. Recognize the power of books as a tool for learning, self-reflection, and personal transformation.

....

....

....

....

....

*Note for thought**

Reading a physical book, whether it's a captivating story or a book full of interesting facts, has many benefits for personal growth and well-being. When you dive into a story, you can escape to new worlds, meet fascinating characters, and expand your imagination.

Non-fiction books give you knowledge about different topics, helping you learn and understand the world better. Reading also keeps your mind active, improves your thinking skills, and helps you remember information. It can even make you more empathetic by allowing you to see things from different perspectives.

Reading is a great way to relax and reduce stress, providing a peaceful break from your daily life. So, grab a book, explore new horizons, and enjoy the many advantages that reading brings to your life.

There are many great books out there! Personally, a book which made a lasting impression on me is a coffee table book by "Nicole Summers" and named "Floriography Birth Month Flowers: The complete book about Birth months flowers the Victorian language of flowers" Available online or on request from bookstores.

"Have you ever tried adult colouring as a form of relaxation or self-expression? If so, what was your experience like and how did it make you feel? If you haven't tried it yet, what intrigues you about adult colouring and how do you think it could benefit you? Take a moment to reflect on your past or potential experiences with adult colouring and consider incorporating it into your self-help journey as a tool for relaxation, creativity, and mindfulness."

....

....

....

....

Note for thought *

Engaging in adult colouring can bring many benefits for your well-being and relaxation. When you colour, you can let your inner artist shine and express yourself using different colours and designs. It helps you focus on the present moment and promotes mindfulness, which means being aware of what you're doing and how you're feeling right now. Colouring has a calming effect on your mind and can help reduce stress and anxiety. It also lets you be creative and express yourself freely, allowing you to try out different colour combinations and artistic styles. Colouring even stimulates your brain and helps improve your concentration and fine motor skills. It's a great way to take a break from screens and technology, giving you a chance to unwind and enjoy a hands-on and therapeutic activity. So, grab your colouring tools, get lost in the beautiful patterns, and experience the relaxing and therapeutic benefits that adult colouring can bring to your life.

I personally have tried and tested many adult colouring books before, there is such a huge market, but I particularly enjoy adult colouring books by Nicole Summers, Grace Williams and Thembi Jones. All available on most online selling sites! Always make sure you have good quality colouring pens and pencils.

Art in wellbeing

How has engaging in art or creative activities positively impacted your mental health and overall well-being.   Reflect on the emotional and therapeutic benefits you have experienced through art, and consider how it has helped you express, process, or cope with your emotions.   If you have not engaged in art activities before, explore how you can incorporate this in your life.

Which art supplies do you feel drawn to: paint, crayons, pencils, or pastels? What makes that medium so appealing to you, and what kind of artwork would you like to bring to life using it? Take a moment to reflect on your preferences and aspirations in the world of art, considering how engaging in this creative process can bring you happiness, self-expression, and a sense of fulfilment. If you haven't explored art before, take some time to think about it deeply and then share your thoughts on which medium you'd like to work with and what kind of artwork you'd like to create.

Art has a unique power to communicate emotions and experiences. If you were to visually express your deepest sadness, how would you depict it through art? Consider the colours, shapes, and symbols that could capture the essence of your soul's burden. Take a moment to reflect on the depth of your emotions and envision how you would translate them into a visual representation. Remember, art can be a powerful tool for self-expression and healing.

Picture yourself with a blank canvas in front of you. Your goal is to create a painting that shows gratitude and the things you're thankful for in your life. How would you bring this to life on the canvas? What colours, objects, and symbols would you use to capture the feeling of gratitude? Take a moment to imagine your artwork and think about what you would paint or draw to express your appreciation for the blessings in your life. Allow your creativity to flow as you explore the visual representation of gratitude through your unique artistic vision.

Self-progression Reflection

What insights have you gained about yourself during this part of the book? Reflect on how music, gardening, books, and art have contributed to your self-discovery journey.

PART SIX

<u>An organised House, enough sleep and mental health.</u>
This last three topics and the final part of this book.

Perhaps you've noticed how your living environment can impact your mental well-being. I certainly have. When my living space is untidy, chaotic, and unclean, I find it difficult to concentrate and my motivation suffers as a result.

Cleaning up and maintaining a tidy living area does require effort, but the rewards are truly worth it. If you delve into the concepts of minimalism and decluttering, you'll discover that getting rid of excess belongings can bring about mental clarity and peace.

In the final part of this book, we will explore the link between an organized living space, sufficient sleep, and mental health. By addressing these areas, you can create a harmonious environment that supports your overall well-being.

How does the state of your living environment affect your overall well-being and mindset? Take a moment to reflect on the impact of a tidy and organized house on your mental and emotional state. Consider how a clutter-free space can promote a sense of calm, clarity, and productivity. Explore the ways in which maintaining a tidy house can contribute to your overall sense of peace and create a positive living environment.

How do you feel when you enter your home? Pay attention to your emotional response when you step through the door. Does your living space evoke feelings of comfort, relaxation, and a sense of belonging? Or do you experience stress, unease, or dissatisfaction? Take a moment to explore the reasons behind these emotions and consider what changes you can make to create a more positive and welcoming living space that truly feels like home.

Take a moment to assess the state of your home, kitchen, bedroom, bathroom and living space in general. Is it cluttered and disorganized, clean, and tidy, or somewhere in between? Reflect on how your living environment affects your daily life, mood, and overall sense of well-being. Consider the impact of clutter and chaos on your productivity, mental clarity, and stress levels. Explore the benefits of creating an organized and harmonious living space and how it can contribute to a more peaceful and fulfilling life.

Notes for thought *

Having a clean and tidy or at least organised house brings many advantages for our overall well-being. It creates a peaceful and calm atmosphere, reducing stress and helping us feel more relaxed. When our living space is organized, it becomes easier to find things and complete tasks efficiently. A clean house also keeps us healthier by preventing allergens and pests. It gives us a sense of accomplishment and boosts our self-esteem. Plus, a clean and tidy home is welcoming to guests and strengthens our relationships. So, by keeping our house clean and organized, we can enjoy a happier and healthier living environment.

Getting enough sleep

Creating a conducive sleep environment is pivotal for a restful night's sleep. It involves curating a space that's not just functional but also aesthetically pleasing, comforting, and inviting. Soft, gentle lighting and cleanliness can set the stage for a peaceful slumber, while making the bed in the morning prepares it for a welcoming return. Opening a window to allow fresh air and natural daylight to filter in revitalizes the space and ushers in a sense of freshness, creating an environment where the body and mind can truly unwind and rejuvenate.

Sleep Hygiene.

What is your current sleep routine like? Reflect on the quality and duration of your sleep, as well as any challenges or concerns you may have. How does your sleep impact your overall well-being and daily functioning? Consider the factors that contribute to a restful night's sleep and explore strategies for improving your sleep habits.

Reflecting on your sleep patterns and dreams, what are some factors that may be influencing the quality of your sleep? Explore any recurring sleep issues, such as difficulty falling asleep, waking up frequently during the night, or vivid dreams. Consider the impact of lifestyle choices, stress levels, and sleep environment on your sleep and dreams. How do your sleep and dreams affect your overall well-being and daily life? Take a moment to delve into your sleep experiences and identify any changes or strategies that can promote restful sleep and enhance your dream state.

How does the environment in your bedroom, including the bedding, impact your sleep quality and overall well-being? Reflect on the comfort, cleanliness, and ambiance of your sleeping space. Consider the role of factors such as the mattress, pillows, sheets, and overall tidiness in creating a relaxing and restful atmosphere. How can you improve the comfort and tranquillity of your bedroom to enhance the quality of your sleep? Take a moment to explore any changes or adjustments you can make to create a sleep-friendly environment that promotes deep and rejuvenating rest.

....

....

....

....

....

....

Note for thought *

During my time in practise, I often encounter individuals who complain about their inability to sleep at night. However, when I inquire about their sleep patterns, I discover that they tend to sleep in until late morning, take afternoon naps, and go to bed after midnight. In such cases, it becomes essential to reprogram the body and mind for better sleep. I suggest establishing a consistent sleep schedule, aiming to go to bed around 11 pm and waking up no later than 7 am. By going through a full day without sleep, you will naturally feel tired at night, allowing your body to find its ideal bedtime. If needed, you can incorporate a short afternoon nap, not exceeding an hour and preferably take before 2 pm or 3 pm. It is crucial to avoid activities that keep the mind stimulated, such as playing games or continuous scrolling, as they can contribute to anxiety and restlessness. Additionally, maintaining good sleep hygiene, such as keeping the bedroom tidy, having fresh bedding, and minimizing artificial light sources, including avoiding having a TV in the bedroom, can greatly enhance the quality of your sleep.

Mental health

I intentionally saved the topic of mental health for the final part of this book.

It often happens that through the process of self-discovery, individuals can uncover insights about themselves that can lead to resolving long-standing issues they have carried with them. By delving into their mental health, they can gain a deeper understanding of themselves and find ways to address and heal from these challenges. This self-reflection and growth can have a transformative impact on their overall well-being and contribute to a more fulfilling life.

Regrettably, in our modern society, individuals are often prescribed medication as quick solution to numb issues, leaving the underlying problems unaddressed. No one explaining or encourage the individual to experience pain, anxiety, and normal human feelings to solve a problem.

Consequently, people continue to live with various diagnoses, unaware that the key lies in addressing the root cause and understanding the reasons behind their feelings. By normalizing and explaining emotions, individuals can resonate with their experiences, effectively address their issues, and work through their feelings. However, it is unfortunate that often, they are simply prescribed more and more medication, without truly resolving the underlying concerns.

Taking care of our mental health and addressing general life issues is crucial for our overall well-being. Mental health encompasses our emotional, psychological, and social well-being, and it affects how we think, feel, and act. It is important to prioritize self-care, seek support when needed and develop healthy coping mechanisms.

Addressing life issues involves facing challenges, setting goals, and making positive changes in various areas of live, such as relationships, career, and personal growth. By nurturing our mental health and addressing life issues, we can cultivate resilience, find balance, and lead a more fulfilling and meaningful life.

It is a continuous journey of self-discovery, self-care, and personal growth that empowers us to navigate life's ups and downs with greater strength and resilience.

How do you take care of your mental health? Think about what you do to prioritize your well-being and keep a positive mindset. Are there specific activities, routines, or support systems that contribute to your mental well-being? Take a moment to explore how you can further enhance your mental health and build resilience to navigate life's challenges.

Are there any specific challenges or areas of your mental health that you would like to address and improve? Take a moment to identify any concerns or areas where you feel you could benefit from additional support or strategies to enhance your mental well-being.

How do you navigate and cope with stress or difficult emotions in your life? Reflect on your current coping mechanisms and consider if there are any healthier or more effective ways you can respond to stressors or manage challenging emotions.

Reflecting on your life experiences and lessons learned, how have they contributed to your mental health and personal growth? Consider the challenges you've overcome, the wisdom gained from difficult situations, and the resilience you've developed along the way. How have these experiences shaped your perspective and helped you cultivate a positive mindset? Take a moment to celebrate the strength and growth that has emerged from your journey.

Reflective summary

What are your reflections on the impact of music, gardening, books, organisation in your house, enough sleep, sleep hygiene, and the effects thereof on mental health, as explored in this last part of the book? How have these elements contributed to your personal growth, well-being, and overall sense of fulfilment? Take a moment to reflect on the significance of these topics and share your insights and experiences.

PART SEVEN

CONCLUSION

WHO AM I?

As you reach the conclusion of this book, take a moment to reflect on who you are and the journey you've embarked on.

Consider the various areas that have been explored, including colours, clothing, shoes, hair, makeup, nutrition, drinks, life experiences, moments of happiness, interests and hobbies, specific interests, role models, people you admire, impactful situations, resilience, personal values, hopes, dreams, and your overall sense of self.

Incorporate the concepts of self-love, self-care, and ways of well-being that have been discussed throughout. Reflect on the beliefs, faith, and spiritual encounters that have influenced your path.

Acknowledge any fears, anxieties, or misbeliefs that may have held you back and consider the positive and negative relationships that have shaped your life.

Express gratitude for the power of music, the beauty of flowers, the wisdom found in books, the therapeutic benefits of gardening, and the importance of mental health.

Draw all these threads together to craft a conclusion about yourself.

Celebrate the growth and self-discovery that has taken place as you have explored these various aspects of your life. Embrace the unique qualities and values that make you who you are.

Remember that reflections and growth is an ongoing journey, and continue to nurture your self-love, well-being, and personal development as you move forward in life.

THIS IS ME!

Summary about myself, what I have learned and discovered through this book. Include all areas addressed. This summary of yourself can take days to complete. Re-visit each chapter's summary and write a review about yourself.

....

....

....

....

....

....

....

....

....

....

Date.....................

Date....................

Date....................

Date....................

www.ingramcontent.com/pod-product-compliance
Lightning Source LLC
LaVergne TN
LVHW070946180726
843512LV00013B/960